# CREATIVE
## EMBELLISHING

# CREATIVE
## EMBELLISHING

Inspiration and techniques for the needle punch machine

TERESA SEARLE

First published in Great Britain in 2010 by
A&C Black Publishers Ltd
36 Soho Square
London W1D 3QY
www.acblack.com

Photography: Michael Wicks
Design: Elizabeth Healey
Commissioning Editor: Janet Ravenscroft
Managing Editor: Kate Haxell
Embellishing inspiration photos: Teresa Searle,
other than those on pages 60 and 86, which are
by Michael Wicks

This book was conceived and produced by
Breslich & Foss Ltd, London

A CIP catalogue record for this book is available from the
British Library.

ISBN 978 1 408 11552 7

Printed and bound in China

10 9 8 7 6 5 4 3 2 1

# CONTENTS

The embellisher is one of the latest machines to appeal to the contemporary textile enthusiast. It has great potential for exploring structure, pattern, colour and texture and exciting effects can be created quickly.

# INTRODUCTION

I first encountered an embellishing machine at a textile workshop and was immediately struck by its simplicity. I felt that its ability to create unique textures offered a huge amount of potential for extending the way I work with many materials.

All the embellishing machines available work in a similar way to a sewing machine, but they use no thread. Instead, they have a set of barbed needles that push fabrics, fibres or yarns together. Depending on the structure and weight of the fabric, the machine may also distort and pull fabrics to create texture and pattern. Many textile artists and designers are now introducing embellishing (also called needle punching) to their repertoire of skills and processes to enhance and complement existing skills in stitching, printing, felting and knitting. Whatever your previous experience or current textile practice, you will find a place in your studio for this addictive machine.

Experimental knitters will enjoy using the embellisher to create innovative yarns from fabrics and fibres, to decorate hand- and machine-knitted garments and to find uses for odds and ends of yarns collected over the years.

Quilters and embroiderers can create textural surfaces that can be further embellished with machine and hand stitches.

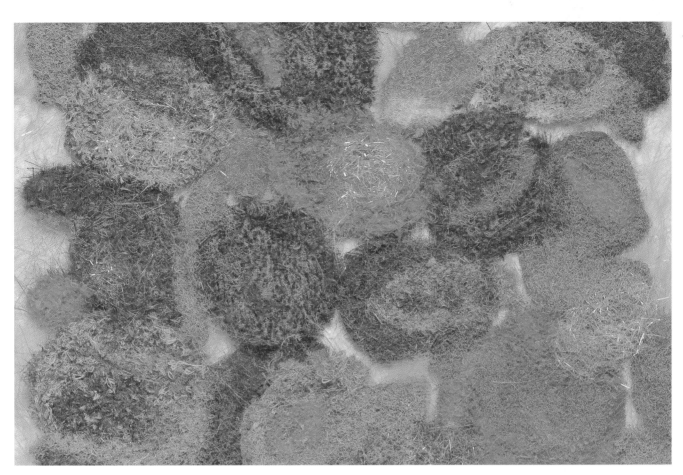

If you have practised free-motion embroidery, you will be
familiar with the movement of the fabric under the needles.

Felters are able to make felts from wool tops and develop
ways of using the machine to innovate and extend their practice.
Consider embellishing hand-made felts with fabrics and threads.

Printers and painters can use the embellisher to add texture:
try combining fine, hand-painted silk with felt and other fibres
to add a new dimension to your work.

Recyclers will love trying out scrap and vintage fabrics, as well
as upcycling existing garments. 'Upcycling' means recycling an
item creatively into something of even greater value, not
necessarily in a monetary sense, but also aesthetically.

However you choose to use the marvellous embellisher
machine, I hope you will enjoy using it as much as I do.

**Teresa Searle**

# GETTING
## STARTED

Other than the embellisher machine itself, you need no special tools or materials to make the projects in this book. Raid your sewing and crafts stash for fabrics, trims, beads, threads, buttons and yarns and you will be ready to start work.

**All kinds of materials can be used on the machine, and this is one area where there is a great deal to be discovered by you. Different combinations of diverse types of fabric are particularly exciting for creating combinations of colour, pattern and various textures.**

# FABRICS

Lightweight and soft fabrics are the most suitable, as harder and thicker fabrics risk breaking expensive embellisher needles. Not all fabrics bond together particularly well and some fabric combinations are much more successful than others.

I prefer to use natural fibres, such as wool, cotton and silk, for their inherent tenacity.

Fabrics can be manipulated before they are worked on the embellisher. Try the scrunch drying method (see Scrunch-drying Fabrics, page 20), or you may want to iron in a series of random pleats. Manipulation of gauzes and muslins or shredding by hand to pull away fibres on fabrics such as dupion silk (see left), are also effective preparation techniques.

Here are a variety of materials that are particular favourites of mine and that feature throughout the book. Many online companies can supply these types of fabric in small quantities or packs designed for embroiderers and quilters.

## SILKS

Silks are my favourite fabrics to use on the machine, as they are strong enough to stand up to the process and can be manipulated beautifully. Many silks provide delicious loops and tufts on the surface when punched onto the back of a fabric. Look for silks such as organza, chiffon, dupion, velvet and habotai in specialist, bridal and Asian fabric shops.

Chiffon fabrics made from silk, or more affordable viscose, also behave wonderfully, ruffling and disintegrating into gorgeous textures. Viscose chiffon comes in a glorious array of colours.

Shot silk fabrics have one colour for the warp and another for the weft, creating iridescent effects. They

**CHIFFON AND LIGHTWEIGHT FABRICS**
*Silk and viscose chiffon fabrics, organzas and habotai silk.*

can be particularly effective under the embellisher machine. Metallic varieties are well worth experimenting with.

Silk velvets, particularly those that are shot, work well on the embellisher, puckering and ruching as well as revealing the fibres from which they are made. Velvet is expensive but a small quantity, mixed with other fabrics, can be enough for a project.

**SILK VELVETS**
*These can be woven from one or two colours to make plain or shot fabrics.*

Printed, patterned silks are also interesting materials. Vintage clothing dealers may have silk scarves and clothing that are ideal for recycling with the aid of the embellisher.

## NATURAL FIBRES

Fabrics such as cotton gauze, organdie, muslin and scrim, provide matt textures and layers. Loosely

**SHOT SILK**
*This type of fabric is woven with two different-coloured threads.*

**NATURAL FIBRES**
*Natural fibres in natural colours.*

# YARNS
## AND THREADS

### YARNS

Yarns of all kinds can be used to add line and detail to work. Due to the resurgence of knitting, there is a huge variety of yarns now on the market, many of which are suitable for use on the embellisher machine.

Woollen yarns work particularly well due to their natural ability to attach to wool and other fabrics. They have the added attraction of being felt-able by hand or washing machine techniques, producing ruched effects (see To Felt Or Not To Felt, page 23).

You can also find interesting, textured mixes, such as wool and silk. Hand-spun and space-dyed yarns are effective, though expensive, choices. Tapestry yarns, used for needlepoint, offer a wide range of colours in small amounts.

### THREADS

Threads punched onto fabric with the embellisher machine can add fine detail in linear form if applied to the surface, or loops and tufts if applied from the back.

Polyester sewing threads, viscose and silk embroidery threads are all rewarding to use, though anything you may have in your thread box is worth trying.

**YARNS AND THREADS**
*Above, knitting yarns. Below left to right, silk threads; rayon embroidery threads; tapestry yarns.*

Embellished fabric benefits greatly from the addition of other elements such as stitch, braids, buttons and beads. I spend time collecting these for craft work in general, and all find their way into embellished projects.

# ADDING DETAIL

## WITH STITCH, BRAIDS, BUTTONS AND BEADS

### BUTTONS

I get a great assortment of modern and vintage buttons from charity shops, antique markets and friends who know how much I appreciate such things. Searching through your collection for just the right button is always a treat!

### TRIMS

Simple and nostalgic braids such as ric-rac and lace can be applied by hand or by sewing machine. They are usually a little too thick to be applied with the embellisher, but some finer lace trims would be suitable.

### THREADS

Hand and machine stitch are both very effective ways of adding detail with all kinds of threads. As well as those threads suggested for adding punched detail (see Threads, opposite), stranded and perlé embroidery threads and linen threads can all provide lovely stitch elements.

### BEADS AND SEQUINS

Widely available in all shapes, colours and sizes, beads and sequins are perfect for highlighting areas of embellished projects.

Build up a collection that you can dip into to find the right selection whenever you need it. Jewellery projects in this book use a variety of beads bought from specialist beading shops and online suppliers.

**DECORATIVE DETAILS**
*Above, buttons. Below left to right, seed and bugle beads; ric-rac trims; linen threads.*

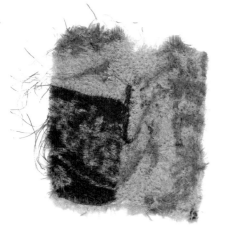

It's best to view the embellisher machine as principally for texturising and manipulating fabrics. It has limited use for constructing useful and practical items, which will usually need additional processes such as hand or machine stitch or the use of bonding, to make them practical on an everyday basis. The embellisher merely pushes fibres together – but as this takes place, wonderful and unexpected things can happen.

# WORKING
## CREATIVELY

Experimentation and imagination are the keys to creativity. Try as many combinations of fabrics, fibres and yarns as possible, recording your findings and making notes on how the work was done.

Different kinds of fabric will behave in quite diverse ways. For example, felted and woollen fabrics are very stable and hold together well. Many finer fabrics will shrink rapidly or disintegrate, so recognise this and use it to your advantage.

Be adventurous, but not foolhardy with outlandish materials or too many layers: broken embellisher needles can be the expensive result of an over-inquiring mind. I rather regret my experiments with paper from the shredder!

You will very likely have other textile skills, such as knitting, crochet, hand and machine embroidery or felting, with which the embellishing process can be combined – adding myriad possibilities to what you can create. Adopt an open attitude to what is produced on the machine. You won't always get what you expect, but you may produce something that can be developed further or in another direction for other projects.

Try not to over-embellish your work. Areas left un-punched can be interesting and may help to produce a more three-dimensional and textured effect.

Use a digital camera to record your progress. A macro setting is useful for capturing textures close up. If you are over-zealous during the

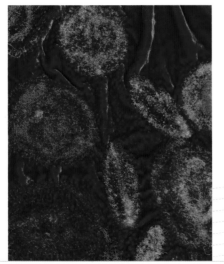

punching process, you can review your work and decide not to go as far next time.

The back of a sample may be more interesting than the front. If you turn over a piece you will find tufts and loops from where the needles have pushed the fibres through the background fabric. Experiment with different combinations of fabrics and fibres to produce beautiful and subtle effects. Record both sides of the fabric with a scanner, photocopier or camera so that you can recall your work at a later date

Use a pinboard to help record, develop and evaluate your ideas. Gathered research, fabrics and samples can live side by side, on daily view to spark off great ideas and further developments. Your pinboard can be recorded with digital photography as it changes and it will help you to remember how your various ideas progressed.

Mistakes are often the key to another creative path and you might just discover something that has a great deal of potential. For example, if you over-punch a sample, it may

weaken and become fragile. It could then be worked further and torn by hand before being reassembled on the machine into an unexpected creation. This was how the layered piece opposite below right was created.

If you make a mistake and apply a piece of fabric that you feel does not look right, it is normally very easy to peel it off. The partially worked fabric can often be applied again, or kept for another sample to produce an even more disintegrated and manipulated look.

## EMBELLISHING INSPIRATION

Throughout the book photographs are shown to illustrate where the inspiration for the various embellished pieces came from.

Photos and drawings, plants in your garden, objects in your home and materials you have already collected can all inform your work.

Collect all forms of visual information on pattern, colour and texture that can be translated into fabrics, fibres and experimental techniques.

Look at the work of other artists using the machine. Search online for blogs and photographs of work that may inspire you. There is a community of all kinds of textile artists sharing work they have made.

## TO FELT OR NOT TO FELT?

If you have created a punched fabric that contains wool fabric, yarn or fibres, it may be beneficial to try treating it with a wet-felting process to change or enhance the textures. Do bear in mind that the resulting fabric might be a disappointment, so take an experimental attitude and make samples first before investing time and money in the final piece!

The wool elements will shrink and felt, as well as embed themselves into any background fibres. They may also create a ruched effect, depending on the fluidity of the background fabric. However, you might lose some of the more delicate textures that have been created by the needles, so you need to make an aesthetic choice.

To felt fabrics, wash them on a hot wash in the washing machine, using your usual detergent. The temperature will depend on the wool type, but for wool tops and most wool yarns, 30°C should be adequate. If this is not effective, try washing your sample again at a higher temperature, up to 60°C. Don't forget that the temperature may also affect the other fabrics in the piece.

In the sample shown as the background of this page, wool tops and yarn were punched onto a piece of muslin curtain fabric. Delicate textures have been created by the needles on the wool and the surrounding areas of the muslin and it has ruched a little.

The inset sample, opposite, shows the same piece once it has been felted in the washing machine. The wool fibres and yarn have felted and the ruched effect has been accentuated, but some of the more delicate textures created by the needles have been washed out.

## FELTING KNITWEAR AND BLANKETS

Knitwear and blankets felted in the washing machine can make good bases for your projects, though used as a top layer they tend to lose the felted texture. Charity shops are a good source for both: look for items in pure wool such as lambswool, cashmere or Shetland wool and ensure that they have not been treated to be machine washable.

Put the items in the washing machine with your usual detergent (I use an eco-friendly one as it is gentler on the fabric and the colour), and set the machine to a long, hot wash. The temperature will depend on the wool type: lambswool and cashmere may felt at 30°C, but a higher temperature of 60°C might be needed for Shetland wool.

## DYEING AND FELTING IN THE WASHING MACHINE

Woollen knitwear and blankets can be dyed in the washing machine using commercial dyes intended for the purpose. The hot water required for the dyeing process will also felt the fabrics at the same time.

## CARE OF FABRICS

As the fabrics created on the embellishing machine are so delicate, washing is not recommended. For some more stable fabrics, especially ones that have subsequently been felted in the wash, dry cleaning may be an option. You could also consider making some pieces detachable, such as the flowers on the Sleeveless Top on page 91.

# FABRICS
## AND FIBRES

In this chapter we look at the basic techniques for creating embellished fabrics and yarns. You will learn how to use wool and silk fibres to create simple designs, fabrics and yarns that will form the basis for many projects.

Wool fabrics are ideal when you're learning to use the embellisher machine: they bond together well and are stable, resisting buckling and ruching. (These are effects you may not want to deal with straight away, but you can capitalise on them as you gain more experience.) Woollen fabrics and felts are also fairly strong and do not disintegrate easily in the way some more fragile fabrics do.

# SIMPLE
## PUNCHED FABRIC

Take care not to choose fabrics that are too thick or dense for your machine to cope with easily. Broken needles are frustrating and expensive to replace.

The finished fabric could be developed to make a handbag, cushion or table runner. Turn to page 20 for finishing techniques, including applying interfacing to prevent motifs easily pulling off.

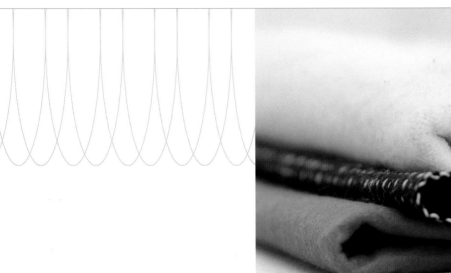

**YOU WILL NEED**
- ☐ Red commercial felt
- ☐ Black and white wool tweed for background
- ☐ Natural-coloured blanket fabric

**EQUIPMENT**
- ☐ Embellisher machine
- ☐ Templates on page 126
- ☐ Paper for templates
- ☐ Pins
- ☐ Small, sharp scissors
- ☐ Spray fabric adhesive and old newsapaper (optional)

1 Photocopy the templates and cut them out to make paper patterns. Alternatively, experiment with cutting and folding paper to make your own flower and star motifs.

2 Pin the patterns to the red felt. Cut out six large and four small motifs, or as many as you need if you plan to make a specific object or project with the finished fabric.

3 Cut circles of blanket fabric; small circles to fit into the middle of red motifs and larger circles to sit between motifs. Arrange the motifs and circles on the tweed fabric and pin them in place. You could also use spray adhesive to temporarily hold the fabrics together.

4 Punch over the surface of the fabrics to join them. If you have used

pins to secure the motifs, remove them as you go, before you get too close to them. Move the fabric around under the needles constantly to punch all over the surface of each motif, paying particular attention to the edges to make sure that they are securely bonded to the background.

1

2

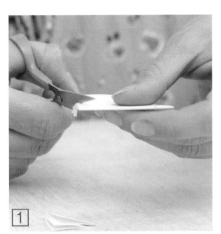

3

4

*embellishing inspiration*

*This felt fabric was inspired by a photograph of an old boat. Its worn surface and subtle colours translate well into the layered construction of felt.*

**You can construct fabrics from scratch using the embellisher machine and fibres such as wool and silk tops. This is an alternative to traditional felt-making processes for making small felt pieces. These pieces can then be developed with the addition of other materials and processes (see Flower Fascinator, page 80; Sea Shell Bowl, page 86; and Vintage Flower Bowl, page 91).**

# FABRIC
## FROM FIBRES

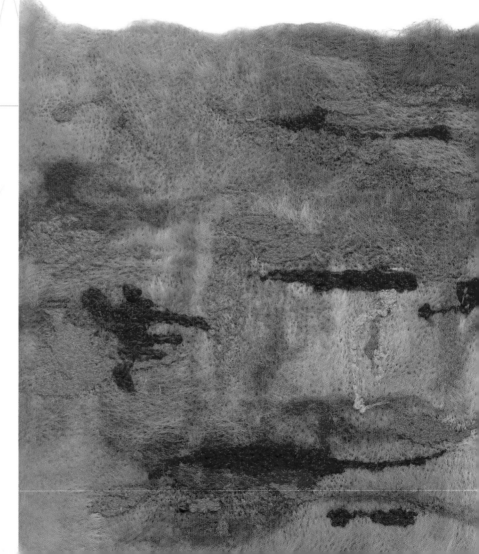

### YOU WILL NEED
- Wool tops in a selection of colours
- Other fibres, such as silk tops

### EQUIPMENT
- Embellisher machine
- A piece of coarse nylon net a little larger than the piece of fabric you intend to make
- An extension table fitted to your machine allows larger pieces of felt to be made easily

## LAYERING THE WOOL TOPS

1 Pull off lengths of wool tops approximately 10cm (4 in.) long and lay them on the work surface. Add overlapping rows to cover an area slightly larger than the piece of felt you wish to make. As you are doing this, build up pattern using different colours of tops. The area the tops cover must be larger than the desired piece of felt as the fibres will shrink once they have been punched. A 30cm (12 in.) square is recommended when trying out the process.

2 Pull off more short lengths and lay them on top of the first layer, but at right angles to it. Again, place the lengths of tops in overlapping rows. Keep in mind your final design as you work, building blocks of colour with different-coloured wool tops.

3 Add a third layer of tops running in the same direction as the first layer. Take care not to make the fabric too thick at this stage, though the machine will reduce the thickness considerably once it has packed down the fibres.

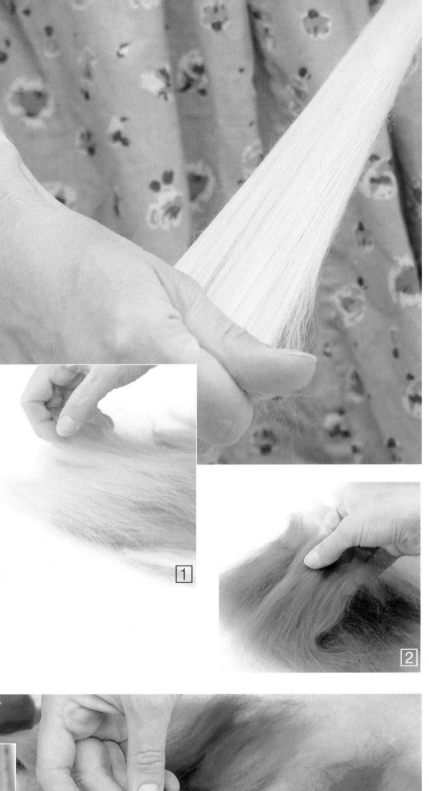

4 Lay the piece of net over the surface of the stack of wool tops. Using your hands, press the fibres as flat as possible, pressing down on the net but not moving your hands from side to side, because this can easily disturb the arrangement of the layers.

5 Following the instructions in the manual, raise the presser foot on your embellisher machine to its maximum height.

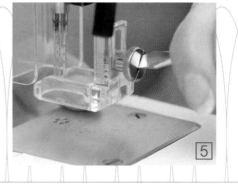

## PUNCHING THE FIBRES

1 Carefully lift the pile of fibres, supporting it underneath with your hands, and slide it under the needles. Start to punch over the surface, punching through the net. At this stage the aim is to bond the fibres loosely, so do not punch too much in any one area in case you integrate some of the net into the fabric by mistake.

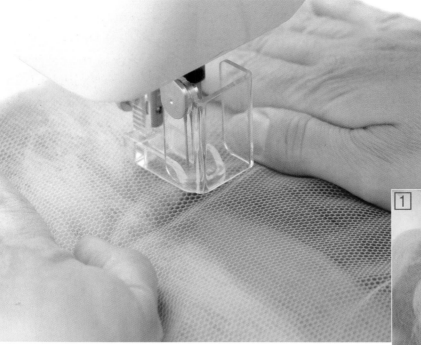

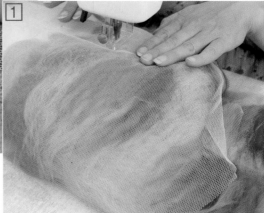

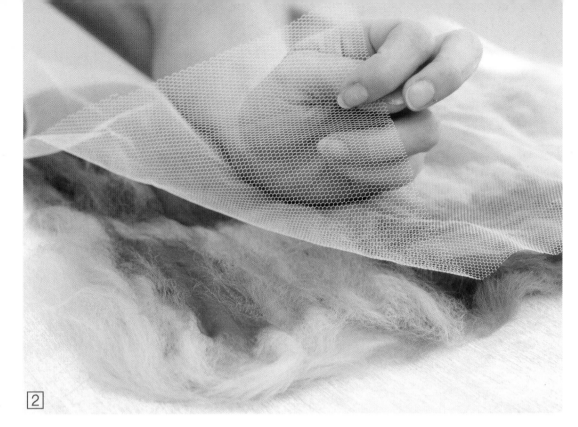

2

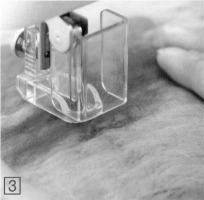

3

2 Once the fibres have started to cling together, remove the net.

3 Continue to punch the wool tops, working alternately on both sides, until the felt fabric is the required density. If you want to make a tidier edge to your piece of felt, fold in the loose fibre edges and punch to neaten them.

4 Add further pieces of wool tops to the front and back of the felt to create gentle changes in colour. Embellishing from the back pushes small amounts of fibre to the front, creating subtle marks and shading. Apply small tufts of silk tops to the fabric to create further detail and variation in surface texture.

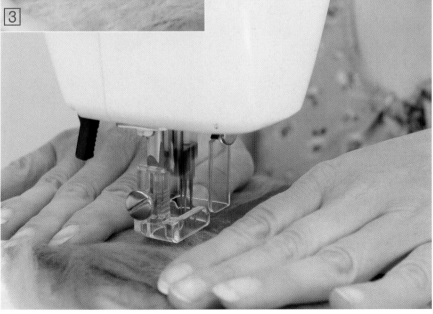

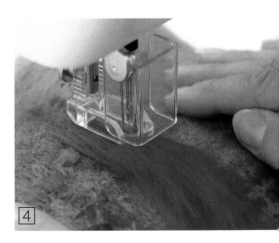

4

Here we explore a range of experimental yarns made with wool tops and fabrics, as well as customising commercial yarns by adding fabrics and fibres. The yarns produced are chunky and can be time-consuming to make, but they knit up quickly on large needles and the big stitches show off the textures to best effect. The thickness of the yarn and the time it takes to make, mean that these stunning yarns are best used for making accessories, such as scarves and bags, rather than full-size garments.

# MAKING
## KNITTING YARNS

*Entangled sweet peas were the inspiration for this embellished yarn.*

## SWEET PEA
### YARN

Wool tops and chiffon fabric are the materials used for this project.

**1** Draw off lengths of tops about 1cm (¾ in.) wide. 'Spin' the fibres into loose-twist yarn by rubbing the lengths between the palms of your hands.

**2** Place each twisted length under the embellisher needles and start to punch it. Move the yarn from side to side as well as backwards and forwards along its length. About every 10cm (4 in.), stop and twist the yarn further. To join lengths, overlap and twist the ends then punch them together. Continue until you have a manageable length of approximately 3m (3 yd) of punched yarn.

**YOU WILL NEED**
- Wool tops in green-grey
- Viscose or silk chiffon in a selection of pinks and greens

**EQUIPMENT**
- Embellisher machine
- Small, sharp scissors
- Rotary cutter, ruler and mat (optional)

3 Cut strips of chiffon measuring approximately 15 x 1.5cm (6 x ⅝ in.), using all the colours. You can fold the fabric and use a rotary cutter to cut the initial lengths, then trim them into shorter pieces with scissors.

4 Work along the length of the wool yarn, twisting and wrapping a strip of fabric around the yarn then punching it in place. Cover all the punched wool tops with fabric in this way.

5 To make the flowers, cut lengths of fabric measuring 4 x 24cm (1½ x 9½ in.). Fold a length six times to make a 4cm ((1½ in.) square, and then fold that square into quarters. Cut out a petal shape and open up the folds to create six flowers.

6 Punch flowers onto the yarn every
10–15cm (4–6 in.) along its length.
Take care not to over-punch or the
flowers will disintegrate.

7 To keep the yarn tidy, wrap it
around a piece of card.

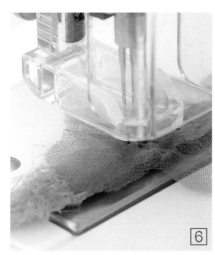

6

7

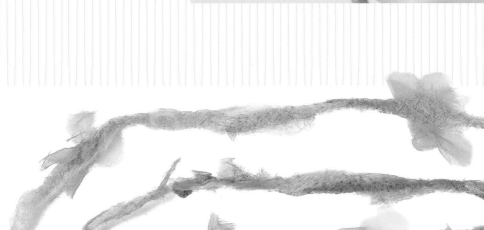

# CUSTOMISED
## COMMERCIAL YARN

This chunky knitting yarn has been
embellished with strips of shot-silk
organza and dupion.

**YOU WILL NEED**
- ☐ Commercial, chunky wool knitting yarn
- ☐ Small amounts of fine fabrics, such as organza, chiffon and dupion, in toning colours

**EQUIPMENT**
- ☐ Embellisher machine
- ☐ Small, sharp scissors
- ☐ Rotary cutter, ruler and mat (optional)

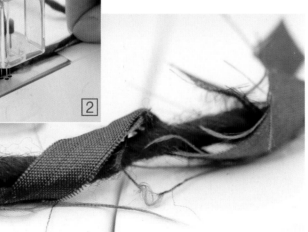

1 Using the rotary cutter or scissors, cut fabrics into strips measuring approximately 15 x 1.5cm (6 x ⅝ in.).

2 Twist and wrap strips of fabric around the knitting yarn and punch them in place in the same way as for Sweet Pea Yarn (see Step 4, page 34). Wind the yarn into a loose ball, ready to use.

# FABRIC
## STRIP YARN

**The distinctive textures and colours produced by lichens growing on the surface of a wall have been translated into a fabric yarn.**

1 Using the rotary cutter or scissors, cut strips of fabric measuring approximately 15–10 x 1.5–2cm (4–6 x ⅝–¾ in.).

2 Take two strips of fabric of different textures and colours and overlap them so that one starts half way along the other. Punch these strips together. The tufts and loops protruding through the fabric emulate the textures of the lichen that inspired this project.

3 When you get to the end of the first strip, add a third strip of fabric to cover the un-punched half of the second strip. Try to select interesting and diverse combinations of texture and colour to get the most interesting effects in your yarn. Continue to punch strips of fabric together until the yarn is the required length. Wind it into a loose ball or onto a piece of card.

**YOU WILL NEED**
- Silk fabrics in a selection of qualities – such as habotai, organza and dupion – and colours

**EQUIPMENT**
- Embellisher machine
- Sharp scissors or rotary cutter, ruler and mat

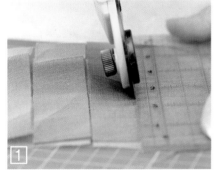

# SAMPLES
## AND IDEAS

A range of simple fabrics and experimental swatches are quick and easy ways to develop first steps into interesting pieces.

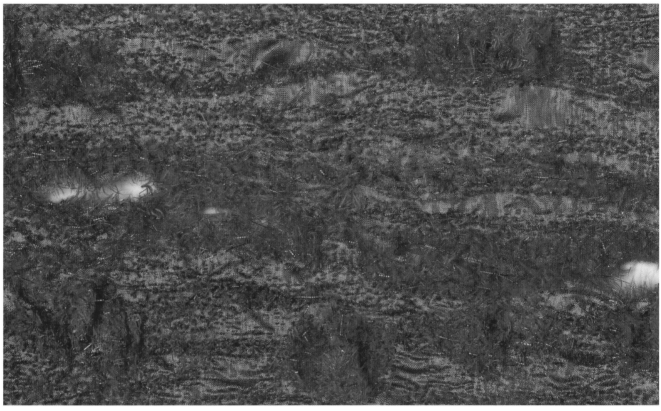

# TEXTURE
## AND PATTERN ON SINGLE FABRICS

Using the embellisher on single fabrics produces subtle textures and patterns. Some embellishers include an adapter for using just one needle and so finer patterns can be created than when using the full set of five or seven needles. A vanishing pen is a useful way of marking out your design before you start to punch the fabric. Suitable fabrics to use alone include silk and polyester organza, cotton organdie and shot silk dupion. You can also distress and age a range of fabrics for use in other projects, such as patchwork.

### PINK METALLIC TEXTURED AND DISTRESSED FABRIC

The shot qualities of this metallic silk fabric have been highlighted by using the embellisher to distress some areas. Manipulation by hand was then used to create holes in heavily punched areas.

## CHUNKY RED SCARF

The yarn for this scarf was made from
recycled fabrics in the same way as the
Fabric Strip Yarn (see page 37), using
strips of silk, cotton and vintage
fabrics. It was rapidly knitted up on very
large needles.

## CREATING SAMPLES

Explore and experiment with as many
types of fabric as possible to discover
their potential. Try combinations of
different fibre types, constructions and
textures. Note which ones are
particularly effective and develop these
further into your own designs or adapt
projects from this book.

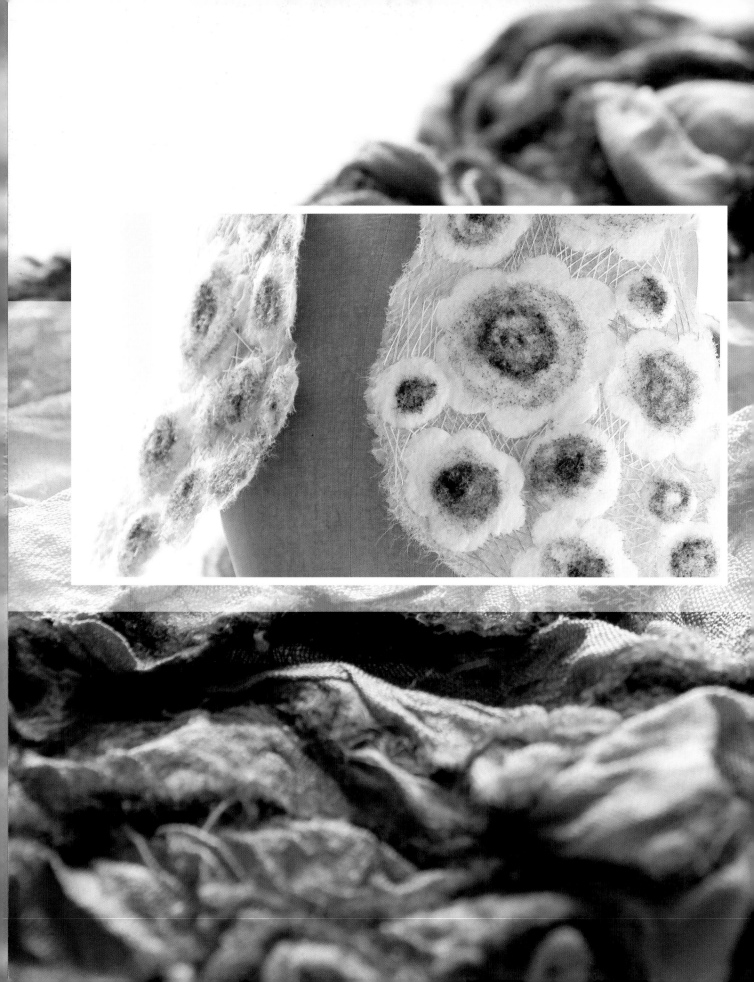

# TEXTURES
## AND LAYERS

Fabrics such as chiffon, muslin, gauze, organza and velvet can be punched together with each other and with various yarns to create rich, textural surfaces for accessories and clothing.

This delicate scarf combines layers of viscose and silk chiffon with hand-spun wool yarn. Look for a yarn that has interesting features, such as variegation in colour or an irregular texture. Viscose chiffon is a good, inexpensive option for a project that requires a large piece of fabric. It comes in many wonderful colours and although it is a natural fibre, it is relatively inexpensive to buy. Alternatively, you could customise a plain scarf bought in a charity shop, but bear in mind that it will reduce in size slightly after being punched.

# CHIFFON
## AND WOOL SCARF

### YOU WILL NEED
- [ ] Length of viscose or silk chiffon in light brown measuring approx 2m x 50cm (2 yd x 20 in.).
- [ ] Matching sewing thread
- [ ] Pieces of red silk or viscose chiffon
- [ ] Hand-spun wool yarn in shades of red/pink

### EQUIPMENT
- [ ] Embellisher machine
- [ ] Scissors
- [ ] Spray fabric adhesive
- [ ] Old newspaper
- [ ] Sewing machine

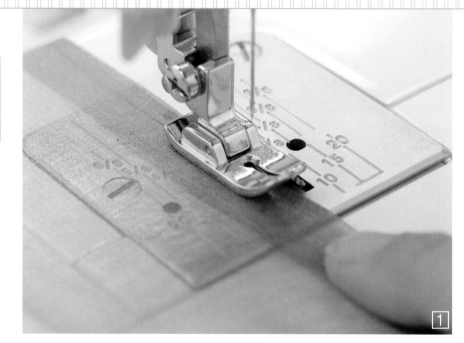

### LAYERING THE CHIFFON
1 Hem the edges of the chiffon using the technique shown on page 21.

[2] Cut out red chiffon flowers varying in size from 10–15cm (4–6 in.) across. A quick way to do this is to take a square of fabric and fold it into eight. Cut a curved but irregular line across with a pair of small, sharp scissors. Remember that as you punch the flowers onto the background, they will shrink to some extent.

[3] Protect the work surface with paper and lightly spray each red chiffon circle with fabric adhesive. Spray one flower at a time then stick each one to the scarf background.

[4] Create a composition using the different-sized flowers at random. It's a good idea to undertake the punching stage within a few days of

using the spray adhesive as it is only meant to be temporary and it soon loses its tackiness.

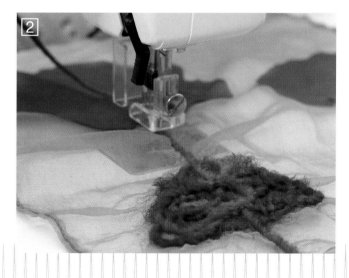

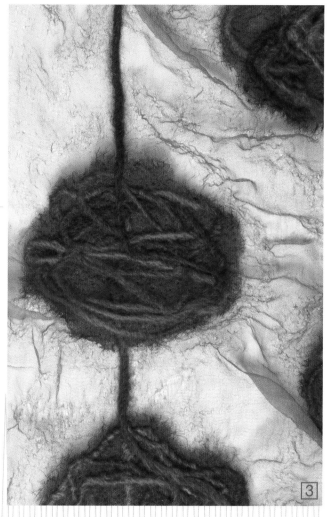

## ADDING THE WOOL YARN

1 Place the scarf under the embellisher machine and lay the hand-spun yarn in a swirling pattern over the first flower. Start to punch with the machine so that the yarn is fused to the layers of chiffon and the surface of the flower is textured.

2 Trail the yarn to the next flower and punch it in place. Then repeat Step 1 to embellish the next flower and the rest of the scarf.

3 Complete the design by punching over the brown chiffon background to create a random texture.

4 Trim the ends of the fabric strip into curves.

## MAKING THE BLOOMS

1 Thread a needle with doubled thread and work a line of running stitch around one curve, along the shorter straight edge and around the second curve. Gather the fabric slightly and secure the thread. The gathered edge is the base of the rose.

2 Re-thread the needle with doubled thread. Roll one end of the strip tightly to form a rose bud. Pass the needle through the base and make a few firm stitches. Roll the rest of the strip more loosely and stitch the base, allowing the rose to form a natural shape. Gather the base

together with several more stitches and finish off the thread firmly.

3 If desired, decorate the rose with crystal beads stitched over the surface. Use a beading needle if necessary and polyester sewing thread. Once you have stitched on the first bead, make a small backstitch

under the bead and pass the needle through the fabric to the next bead position. Alternatively, you can glue on diamanté using small amounts of gemstone or fabric glue. A cocktail stick is useful for applying the glue and a pair of tweezers for positioning the stones.

## GREY SILK AND ORGANZA

Grey silk has been overlaid with
silk organza, then punched from the
back to produce this textured and
looped sample.

## LACE COMBINED WITH TWEED

Wool herringbone tweed has been
layered with vintage-style patterned silks
and a lace fabric, held temporarily with
spray fabric adhesive. Once punched, the
roses and other areas have been
highlighted using stitch. Small seed
pearls have been scattered over the
surface of the lace and vintage diamanté
and pearl buttons add a finishing touch.

*embellishing inspiration*

*The patched and worn wall of a
house with a few last roses
surviving in December has
been translated into lace and
fabric-patch layers.*

## LAYERED FABRIC

The base fabric was created using Angelina fibres ironed between sheets of silicone baking parchment (follow manufacturer's instructions). Strips of various toning fabrics were then punched through to add texture and colour. The fabric was then torn into pieces and reconstructed in layers using fabric glue.

## GREY SILK AND WOOL YARN FELTED FABRIC

Hand-spun wool yarn has been punched in stripes onto silk. It has been felted in the washing machine to further distort the fabric (See To Felt Or Not To Felt, page 23). Finally, the fabric has been scrunch dried (see Scrunch-drying Fabric, page 20) to create even more texture. This fabric could be developed into a scarf or shawl.

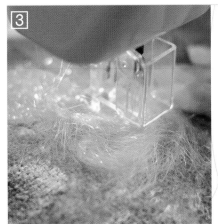

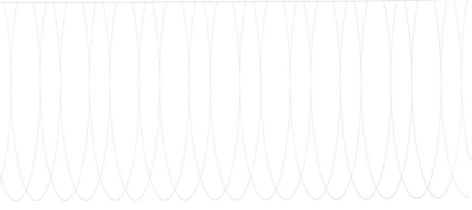

3 Take a small bundle of Angelina fibres, shape it into a circle and embellish it onto the fabric from the back. Keep checking the front to assess the effect. You may wish to apply shot metallic silk organzas as well as other fabrics. Keep working threads, fibres and fabrics through from the back until you are happy with the result.

4 Thread the hand-sewing needle with a doubled length of embroidery thread and make rough star stitches over the surface of some of the flowers, changing the colour of the thread as desired. Embellish over these hand stitches to embed them into the surface.

5 You may then want to stitch beads or sequins in toning colours onto the flowers to catch the light.

2 Pin the felt in place and stitch about 1cm (⅜ in.) in from the edge using straight stitch on the sewing machine. Leave the lovely edges untrimmed to make the most of them. Insert the cushion pad.

**BELOW** *If you prefer a neat edge to the decorative cover, pin the back and front together right sides facing and stitch around 1cm (⅜ in.) in from the edge using straight stitch. Trim the edges to 5mm (1/8 in.) and turn right side out. Roll out the edges with your fingers and press carefully with a steam iron, taking care to iron the edges only. You may iron out some of the carefully created texture if you are over zealous! Insert the cushion pad.*

## MAKING UP THE CUSHION

1 You may find that the embellishing process has altered the dimensions of the cushion cover. Re-measure it and trim the backing pieces of felt cut in Step 1 so that they sit on the embellished fabric about 1cm (⅜ in.) in from the edge. Lay the backing pieces over the embellished piece, wrong sides facing, so that they overlap in the centre.

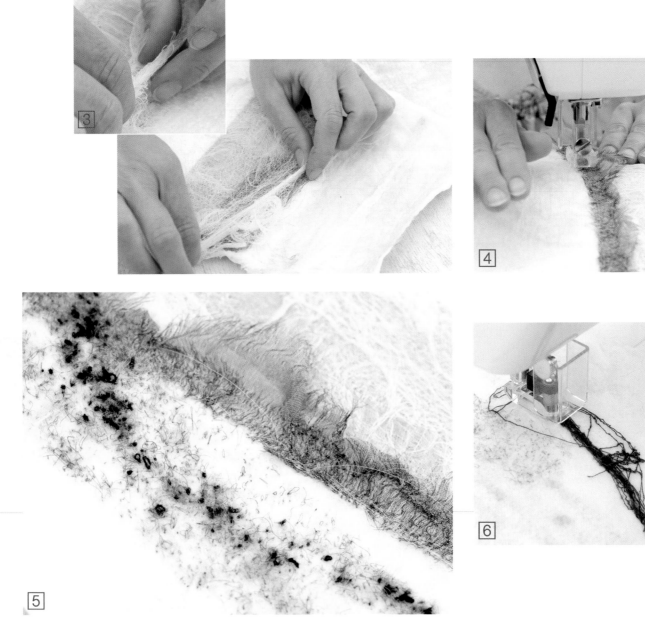

[3] Pull apart the fibres in a piece of cotton gauze and lay it on the surface, approximately halfway down and over the organza and muslin strips. Punch it in place from the right side.

[4] Punch a frayed piece of grey organza onto the surface to represent a hedge.

[5] From the back, apply strips of black and shot grey organza. Check progress on the right side from time to time: you are aiming for subtle loops and tufts to represent bushes and hedgerows covered in snow.

[6] Pull off lengths of black and grey threads and form bundles. Lay them

on the back of the work and punch them through. Check your progress on the right side, where loops will be formed on the surface.

Check the composition and add any additional fabrics and threads to the surface or the back as required.

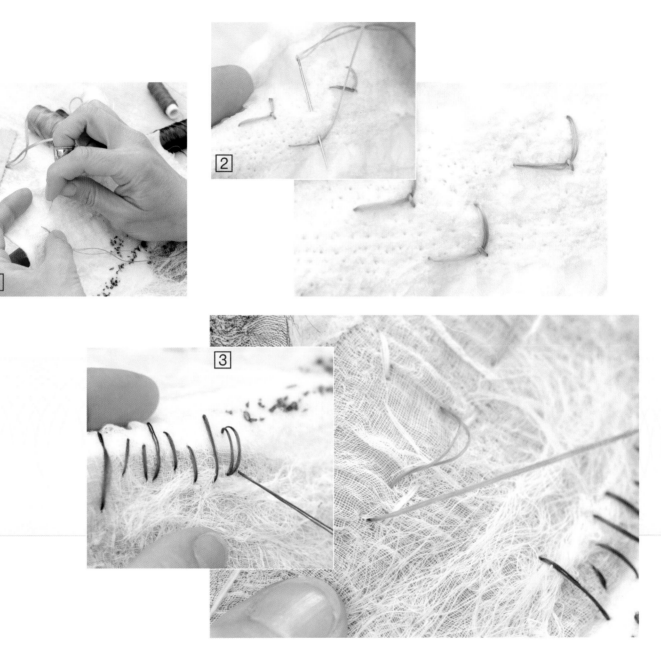

## ADDING EMBROIDERY

1 Use embroidery stitches to add detail to your embellished textile.

2 Use fly stitch in the sky area to indicate birds in flight. Bring the needle and embroidery thread up through the fabric. Take the needle back down approximately 1cm (⅜ in.) to the right and make a slanting stitch coming out between where the needle came out and went back in and 0.5cm (¼ in.) lower: do not pull the needle through.

Slip the loop of thread under the tip of the needle, then pull the needle and thread taut to make a V shape.

Take the needle down through the fabric to make a tiny holding stitch.

3 Work stab and running stitch over the surface in lines to denote fence posts and reeds. Bring the needle and thread up through the fabric and then back down to make random-sized stitches.

# SAMPLES
## AND IDEAS

## SHADES OF GREY

The background to this piece, which was inspired by fabrics of the 1950s, was formed from white felt embellished with various habotai silks and shot silk organzas. Shot and black organza was punched from the wrong side of the fabric to form a subtle looped texture on the surface. Bundles of polyester sewing thread and viscose embroidery threads were then punched onto the surface to create an interesting effect. This fabric could be used to create a striking cushion, but one with a minimalist aesthetic.

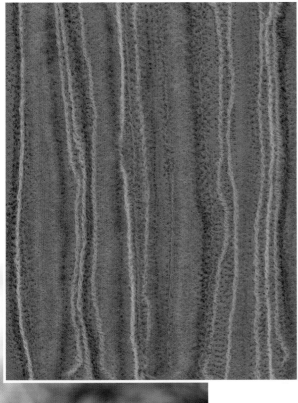

## FELT AND TAPESTRY YARN SWATCH (LEFT)

A commercial wool felt was hand-dyed and embellished from both sides with tapestry wool yarns in various colours. On the right side they present as crisp clean lines; punched from the other side they contrast as fuzzy shadows.

## STAR FLOWER SCARF (BELOW)

This soft tweed scarf was embellished with a silk/wool mix variegated yarn to create stems. Strips of chiffon were punched on to form star-shaped flowers. Finally, bundles of black woollen embroidery threads were embellished onto the flowers to provide detail.

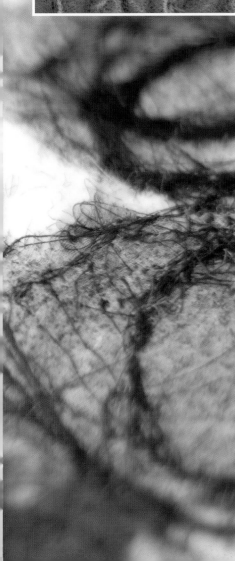

# RUFFLES
## AND TUCKS

This chapter looks at both the decorative effects and structural shaping that can be achieved using the embellisher machine. By manipulating a flat piece of felt you can create three-dimensional items, such as bowls.

Layers of fine fabrics ruffle up beautifully under the embellisher to resemble flower petals. This delicate headpiece capitalises on this effect, which is further enhanced by sequins and beads in toning colours. Consider making the flowers to decorate other projects – such as the Sleeveless Top on page 91 – or as corsages or hair slides. Flower centres could be beaded, sequinned or buttoned.

# FLOWER
## FASCINATOR

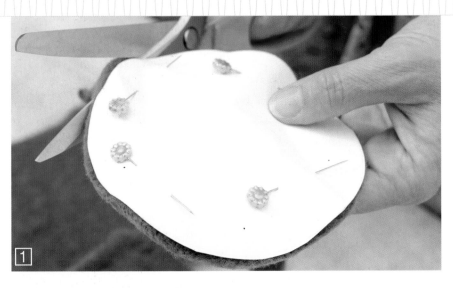

## YOU WILL NEED
- Wool tops in dark grey
- Hat elastic
- Selection of fine fabrics, such as silk dupion, viscose or silk chiffon and silk organza, in toning greys and purples
- Grey/green shot-silk organza

- Matching sewing threads
- Sequins in several shades of pinks and purples
- Small rocaille beads to tone with sequins

## EQUIPMENT
- Embellisher machine
- Nylon net
- Compasses
- Pins
- Hand-sewing needle
- Beading needle (optional)
- Small, sharp scissors

## SHAPING THE BASE

1 Using the embellishing machine, make a piece of felt that measures approximately 15 x 20cm (6 x 8 in.) from the wool tops (see Fabric From Fibres, page 28). If you have an extension table for your machine, you will find it very useful for this stage. Use the nylon net to start off the process and remove it once the fibres have started to bond together. Create a fabric that will hold together when cut; it does not have to be firmer as it will be worked further at the shaping stage. Use the compasses to make a circle template with a 7cm (2¾ in.) radius. Pin the template to the felt and cut out the shape: keep the rest of the felt as the base for the flowers.

**OPPOSITE** *Garden flowers with fluted, layered petals, such as scabious and roses, were the source of inspiration for this charming fascinator.*

*embellishing inspiration*

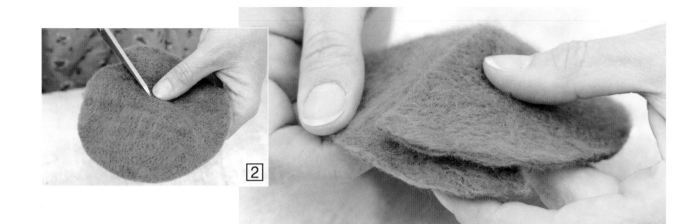

2 Make a cut from the outside edge to the centre of the circle. On the outside edge, overlap the edges by 9cm (3½ in.) to create a shallow cone. 3 Remove the flat bed of the embellisher machine to reveal the free arm. Punch together the overlapped edges of the felt. Working from both sides, punch the circle until it becomes a smooth convex shape. Keep punching until the felt is firm and the seam is invisible.

## MAKING THE FLOWERS

1 Cut six circles, each one approximately 4cm (1¾ in.) in diameter, from the remaining grey felt for the flower centres.

2 From the chiffon, shot dupion and organza fabrics, cut squares ranging in size from 8–12cm (3–4¾ in.). Fold the fabrics into quarters, eighths or sixteenths and cut different petal shapes with small, sharp scissors. Unfold the resulting flower shapes.

3 Arrange the shapes in piles to compose the flowers, ensuring a range of textures and shades for each one. You will need four or five layers for each flower and a total of six complete flowers.

4 Replace the flat bed of the embellisher machine. Lay a grey felt circle in the middle of a single layer of a fabric flower and punch them together. Turn the felt over and punch another fabric layer onto the other side. The punching will cause the fine fabrics to ruffle and form more three-dimensional flower shapes.

A bowl shape can be achieved by cutting, folding and punching the felt over the free arm of the embellisher machine. Part of the machine's base is easily removed to reveal the free arm section: have a look in your machine manual for instructions on how to do this.

# SEASHELL
## BOWL

*embellishing inspiration*

*This bowl was inspired by my collection of seashells. The manipulation of the pale and translucent fabrics echoess the intricate texture of the shells.*

## SHAPING THE BOWL

**1** Using the embellishing machine, make a piece of felt measuring approximately 30 x 30cm (12 x 12 in.) from the wool tops (see Fabric From Fibres, page 28). If you have an extension table for your machine, you will find it very useful for this stage. Use the nylon net to start off the process and remove it once the fibres have started to bond together. Create a fabric that will hold together when cut, but make sure that you do not over-punch it at this stage as it will be worked further when the fabrics are added. Cut the felt into a rough circle. Cut four straight lines, at the compass points, from the edge of the circle to about 5cm (2 in.) from the centre.

**2** Remove the extension table or flat bed from your embellishing machine to reveal the free arm. On the outside edge of the felt circle, overlap the edges of one of the cuts by 5–7cm (2–2½ in.).

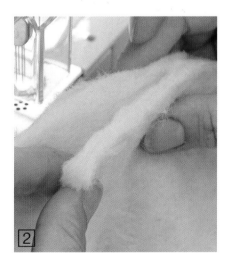

## YOU WILL NEED

☐ White or natural-coloured wool tops
☐ A selection of cream and white fine fabrics and gauzes in cotton and silk, such as muslin, organza and organdie
☐ Small pieces of grey organza or muslin
☐ Fine fabrics that have been treated with the scrunch-drying method (see Scrunch-drying Fabrics, page 20)

## EQUIPMENT

☐ Embellisher machine
☐ Scissors
☐ Nylon net

**3** Slide the overlapped section under the machine and start to punch the layers together to form a dart and so shape the bowl.

**4** Overlap and punch the edges of each of the four cuts in turn until a bowl shape is formed. The edges of the cuts should be punched into the felt so that they are almost invisible.

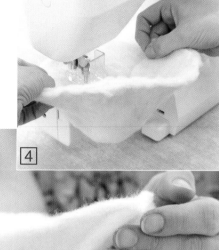

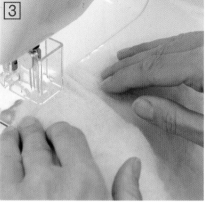

## ADDING FABRICS

**1** Cut wide strips of organza and punch them onto the inside top edge of the bowl. Work around the inside of the bowl, allowing the fabric to ruche and fold in places so that it fits the shape. There is no need to attach it thoroughly as the bowl will also be worked from the outside.

2 Apply strips of darker fabrics as a base layer on the outside of the bowl. These will be tempered by applying lighter fabrics and will appear as a shadow underneath the bowl and as dark tufts on the inside.

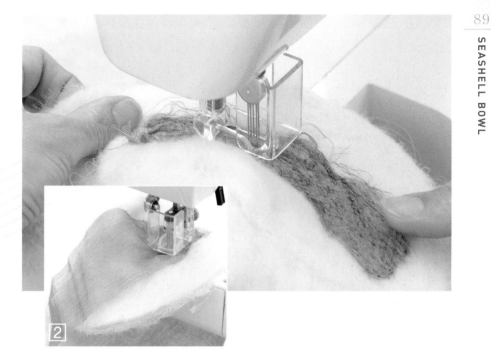

## ADDING FRILLS

1 From your stock of muslins, organzas and chiffons, tear narrow pieces of fabric to create strips with tattered edges. Punch these strips onto the outside of the bowl in overlapping layers. Take care not to over-embellish and avoid the tattered edges so that gentle frills form. Some of the strips can be pleated before they go under the needles of the machine.

2 Using scissors, cut strips of scrunch-dried fabric. Lay them around the outside of the bowl, up to and over the top edge. Punch the strips in place, again avoiding the edges so that frills form naturally. Keep adding strips until the felt base has been covered and a layered effect is achieved.

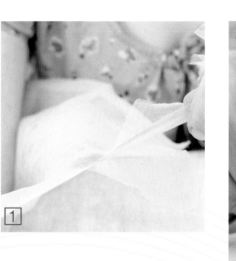

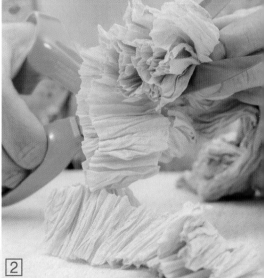

## TUCKS AND RUCHES
### (BACKGROUND)

This simple example shows how intricate tucks and ruching can be achieved by applying fine fabrics, such as organza, muslin and chiffon, onto a firm background, such as felt, Don't use spray adhesive and cut the fabrics about one-third larger than the background to allow for shrinkage as they gather up onto the felt.

Designs can be varied by using different types of fabric and by leaving areas unworked. This can make an interesting base for further work, such as the Seashore Sample on page 92.

# SAMPLES
## AND IDEAS

### VINTAGE-STYLE BOWL

A square of red felt made from wool tops on the embellisher machine has had a patchwork of fabrics embellished onto both sides. Care has been taken to wear away areas to give an aged effect. A four-petal flower shape has been cut from the square and been decorated with ric-rac and buttons. It has then been hand-stitched together, the petals overlapping to make a bowl shape.

### SLEEVLESS TOP DECORATED WITH FLOWERS

This was a lambswool cardigan destined for the recycling bag. Its arms were worn, so these were cut off and the armholes hemmed to make a sleeveless top. The buttons were exchanged for an assortment of vintage ones. A group of blossoms was made in the same way as for the Flower Fascinator (see page 80) and was finished with more buttons instead of sequins. The flowers were then stitched onto the top in a spray on one side. Alternatively, the flowers could be removable. Simply stitch brooch backs to them, making the top easy to wash by hand.

*embellishing inspiration*

*Photos of barnacles, limpets and seaweed taken on a trip to the beach inspired this sample of ruched, ruffled and layered fabrics.*

## SEASHORE SAMPLE

This seashore-inspired piece has fabrics attached in a variety of ways. Some have been allowed to ruffle as they go under the needles, while others have been tucked and folded randomly by hand as they go through the machine. Also attached are strips of scrunch-dried fabrics (see Scrunch-drying Fabrics, page 20) and Suffolk puffs. Further detail has been added using embroidery threads in a variety of textures and stitches, such as stab stitch and French knots.

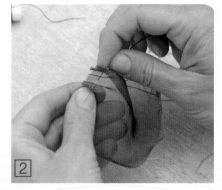

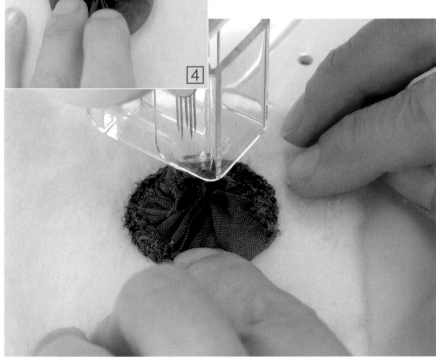

## MAKING AND ATTACHING A SUFFOLK PUFF

[1] Cut a circle from a piece of fine fabric. You can do this by folding and cutting a quarter circle or by using a circle template.

[2] Using polyester thread and running stitch, work a line of running stitch around the edge of the circle.

[3] Pull up the thread to gather the fabric into a puff. Fasten off the thread.

[4] Punch the puff to the background fabric. Embellish around the outside edge only, as the thicker centre may break the needles.

# PATTERN
## AND PRINT

In this chapter we explore how patterned and printed fabric can be used on the embellisher machine. The machine can change a pattern's appearance and character, creating texture and disintegration that can be further enhanced with stitch and other embellishments. I have used a range of contemporary, vintage and computer-printed fabrics in these examples.

This project gave me the opportunity to upcycle a plain, wool tweed skirt by applying flowers cut from vintage fabrics. The look was enhanced by the addition of pink and red ric-rac. Wool is an excellent choice as a base as it doesn't pucker as easily as other fabrics. If it does rumple slightly, pressing with a damp cloth and an iron can rectify the problem. To prevent the motifs pulling away from the skirt with wear and tear, a good tip is to use iron-on interfacing on the back of the floral fabric (see Using Iron-on Interfacing, page 21).

# RETRO
## FLOWER SKIRT

### PREPARING THE FLOWERS

1 Using small sharp scissors, cut a variety of different-sized flowers from the floral fabrics.

## YOU WILL NEED
☐ Wool skirt to upcycle
☐ A selection of vintage and vintage-style thin cotton fabrics with a variety of floral motifs
☐ Narrow red and wide pink ric-rac to go around hem and waist
☐ Sewing threads to match ric-racs
☐ Very lightweight iron-on interfacing
☐ Spray fabric adhesive

## EQUIPMENT
☐ Embellisher machine
☐ Small, sharp scissors
☐ Pins
☐ A dressmaker's dummy is useful for viewing flower positions on the skirt
☐ Old newspaper
☐ Vanishing fabric marker pen
☐ Iron and pressing cloth
☐ Sewing machine

[2] Position and pin the flowers onto your skirt to form a pleasing arrangement. Take your time over this, trying out different options and viewing it from all angles to ensure there are no gaps. A dressmaker's dummy makes this task much easier. Leave enough room above the hem to add the rows of ric-rac.

[3] Un-pin the motifs one at a time and place them on a sheet of old newspaper. Spray the back lightly with fabric adhesive and re-position the motif on the skirt.

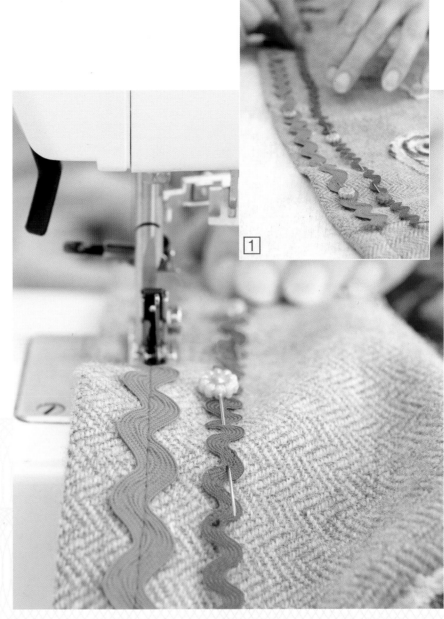

### PUNCHING THE FLOWERS

[1] If the skirt has a lining, make sure it is pulled through the waistband and well away from the main fabric. Place the main part of the skirt under the machine and, one at a time, punch the flowers onto the fabric. Take care not to over-punch, but make sure the flowers are well attached all over and slightly disintegrated to enhance the vintage look.

[2] Turn the skirt inside out. Place the interfacing glue-side down over the backs of the flowers and trace the shapes using the fabric marker pen. Cut the shapes out, place them glue-side down over the backs of the flowers and iron them on, protecting the fabric with the pressing cloth. Don't iron on large pieces across several motifs as it may significantly affect the drape of the skirt.

### ADDING RIC-RAC

[1] Pin on ric-rac in rows around the hemline, overlapping it at the joins. Stitch it on, sewing a straight line down the middle using matching sewing threads and a straight stitch on the sewing machine. Press the skirt using a pressing cloth and steam iron to give a good finish.

This decorative patchwork uses a range of new fabrics and recycled clothing, as well as found scraps. Stitch highlights some of the floral motifs, and the patchwork is finished with lace, braid and buttons.

The great thing about using vintage or vintage-style fabrics is that the embellisher disintegrates them even more, enhancing their aged

# VINTAGE
## PATCHWORK

*embellishing inspiration*

look. Unfortunately this makes the fabric unsuitable for practical applications, so it is best to use these techniques for making decorative or art pieces only.

It's worth doing some tests on the fabrics first, especially the silks, to see how much they will shrink under the machine, and then cutting your pieces accordingly. If you find you have miscalculated when making the patchwork, you can either pull the fabric off and start with a new piece, or add extra bits to cover the gaps and complete your composition. The spray fabric adhesive will reduce the shrinkage considerably, but the textures achieved will be less dramatic.

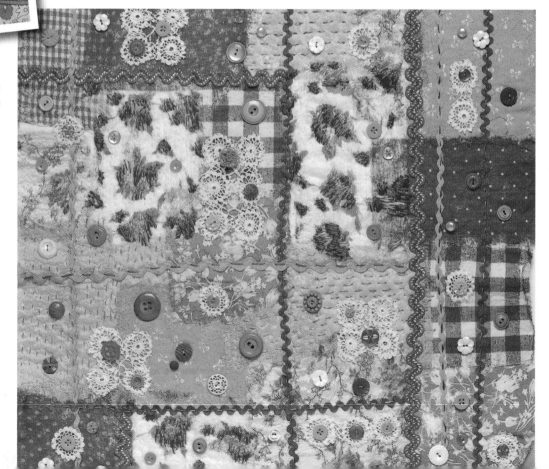

*A quilt made for my partner by his granny when he was a baby inspired the piece. It has memories for both of us and contains many beautiful 1950s dress fabrics, all of which I covet greatly.*

1

## PREPARING THE PATCHWORK

1 Cut a large square of felt the size you would like the patchwork to be. This one is approximately 48 x 50cm (19 x 20 in.) Arrange various-sized pieces of the vintage fabrics on the felt. Aim for a range of patterns and harmonising colours. Make sure that you overlap the fabric pieces beyond the edges of the felt a little, as well as them overlapping each other to allow for possible shrinkage.

## YOU WILL NEED

- ☐ Large piece of fine commercial felt in white or colour to tone fabrics
- ☐ A selection of vintage and vintage-style printed silk and cotton fabrics
- ☐ Hand-embroidery threads
- ☐ Vintage buttons of various sizes and colours
- ☐ Matching sewing threads
- ☐ Ric-rac of various sizes and colours
- ☐ Pieces of lace; here I have used an old lace doily found in a charity shop

## EQUIPMENT

- ☐ Embellisher machine
- ☐ Small, sharp scissors
- ☐ Long quilting pins
- ☐ Spray fabric adhesive
- ☐ Old newspaper
- ☐ Embroidery and sewing needles

2 Use the spray adhesive to bond the fabrics to the felt. Alternatively, use large quilting pins to hold the fabrics in place.

## PUNCHING THE FABRICS

1 Use the embellisher machine to punch all the fabrics onto the felt. As you do so, some fabrics may reduce in size, even if you have used the spray adhesive. If a gap appears, add another piece of fabric over the top.

2 Concentrate the punching further on some areas to disintegrate the fabrics and create a worn effect.

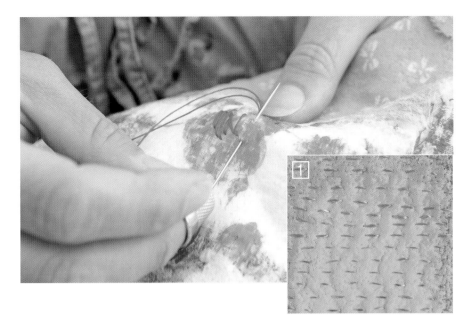

## DECORATING THE PATCHWORK

1 Using the embroidery threads, add hand stitches to some areas. For example, here I have used stab stitch (see page 71) to enhance the rose print and some plain areas have rows of running stitch.

2 Pin the braids and ric-rac onto the patchwork. Either stitch it on with a sewing machine or by hand using decorative running stitch and embroidery threads.

3 Cut small pieces of lace and pin them onto areas of the patchwork. Hand-stitch them in place using polester sewing thread.

4 Finally, sew pretty vintage buttons onto areas of lace and fabric to complete the patchwork.

# SAMPLES
## AND IDEAS

## VINTAGE BUTTON CUFF

This pretty piece of jewellery was created by embellishing a strip of felt with vintage fabrics. It was then embroidered with running stitch and finished with a selection of carefully chosen buttons.

## VINTAGE GREETINGS CARDS

A range of cards was made using scraps of vintage and found fabrics punched onto a felt background. The fabrics were decorated with stitch, ric-rac, lace and buttons. The lilac card features a simple flower created by hand stitching ric-rac into a spiral; braid was used to make a stem. Double-sided tape is an easy way to mount the swatches onto card blanks.

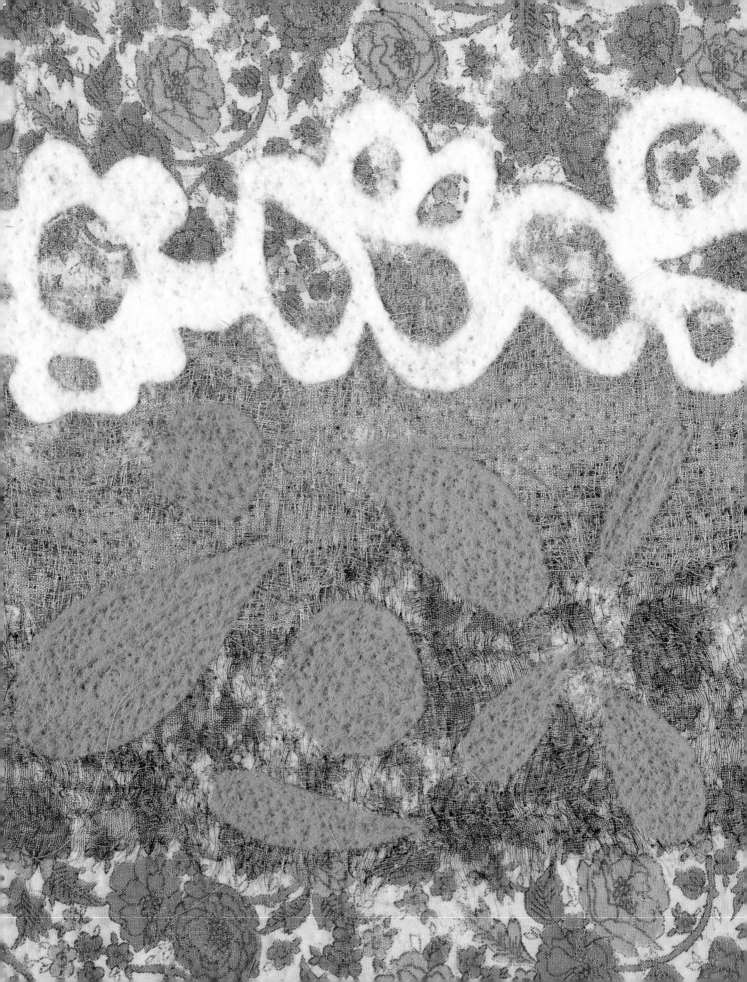

## VINTAGE FABRICS WITH CUT FELT SHAPES (OPPOSITE)

Floral vintage cotton fabric and finer silks were embellished over a felt base. Shapes cut from commercial white and grey felt were layered and punched over the surface.

## TIGER LILY SAMPLE

This sample was based on stories about my grandmother in a family history written by my late father and uncle. I never met my paternal grandmother and it was lovely to find out about our shared interest in textiles and embroidery. The photo and words were extracted from the history and transferred by computer printer onto silk fabric specially prepared for the purpose. The silk was punched onto a felt background and distressed silks and muslins were added to form a border. To enhance the effect, shot organza and silks were applied from the reverse to form loops and tufts on the surface. This piece could be combined with printed fabrics and stitch and be developed into an art quilt based on a family tree.

## PRINT MIXED WITH DISTRESSED FABRIC AND HAND STITCH

Printed silk chiffon and silk recycled from a blouse were distressed with the embellisher and torn in places by hand. The machine was used to apply the fabrics to a felt base. Some parts were avoided to achieve a slightly three-dimensional look. Areas were highlighted with stitch using viscose embroidery threads.

LILY ETHEL GANE

"Tiger Lily"

Lily was an early riser and Monday was devoted to the washing of family clothes and of household items

It was not all work and Lily was able to take up a new interest, embroidery. This she did with wool stitched on Russian crash. She was able to produce some first class work in beautiful colours.

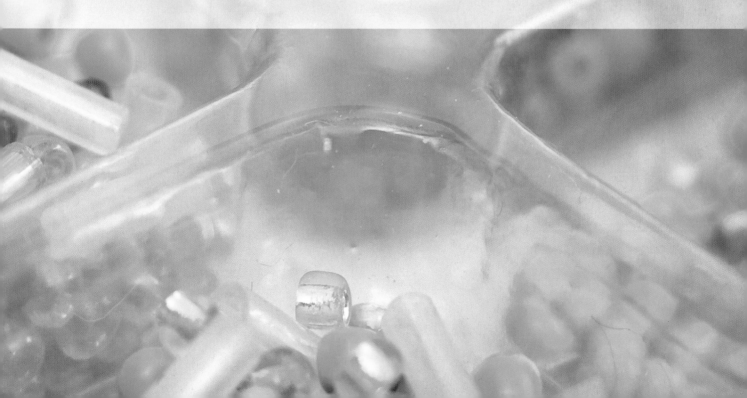

# DETAILS
## AND DECORATIONS

Embellished fabrics provide a gorgeous base for other textile techniques. If you are an ardent hand embroiderer, you will love responding to the textures with a variety of stitches and threads. Machine embroiderers will enjoy developing these fabrics with manipulation and free-motion embroidery. The delicate surfaces look particularly beautiful when beaded in a random, organic way to make the most of the fabric's frayed and uneven qualities.

Embellished fabric is used as a base for manipulation through tucking on the sewing machine and hand-embroidery with a variety of threads. Antique mother-of-pearl buttons and cane handles complete this delicate, encrusted handbag.

The bag has been constructed so that the raw edges are outermost and become a feature. Using cotton muslin as a base not only provides a lightweight backing, but also produces little loops on the right side of the work to create added texture.

# LICHEN WALL
## HANDBAG

*embellishing inspiration*

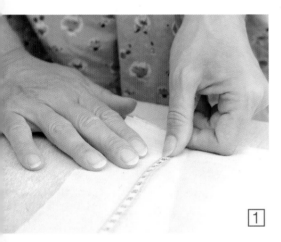

### MAKING THE BAG FABRIC

1 Cut two equal-sized rectangles of backing muslin about 6cm (2½ in.) larger than you want the bag to be. Cut and tear strips of silks, muslins and linens. Make these a little longer than the pieces of backing muslin to allow for shrinkage.

1

*The idea for the textures and colours of this bag came from lichen-covered walls I photographed.*

### YOU WILL NEED
☐ Fine cotton or linen muslin as backing fabric
☐ A selection of textured silk, cotton and linen fabrics.
☐ Silk and cotton muslin fabrics that have been scrunch dried (see Scrunch-drying Fabrics, page 20)

☐ Cream sewing thread
☐ Yellow, grey and cream embroidery threads in a variety of textures, such as viscose and linen
☐ A selection of mother-of-pearl buttons
☐ Plain cotton or silk fabric for lining
☐ Cane or wooden bag handles

### EQUIPMENT
☐ Embellisher machine
☐ Hand-sewing and embroidery needles
☐ Scissors
☐ Pins
☐ Sewing machine

2 Punch the fabric strips onto one of the backing pieces using the embellisher machine. Arrange them in stripes, butted up closely against one another.

3 Punch from the back to create small loops of the backing fabric on the right side of the work.

4 Continue in this way until the piece of muslin is completely covered with fabric strips.

5 Cut additional strips of scrunch-dried fabrics and punch these on to create more stripes. Repeat to cover the second backing piece.

2

3

5

4

## DECORATING THE FABRIC

1 Thread your sewing machine with cream sewing thread. Fold the fabric at right angles to the direction of the fabric stripes and stitch a tuck about 5mm (¼ in.) from the folded edge. Repeat four times to make five irregularly spaced tucks. Repeat the process on the second piece of fabric. Compare the two pieces to ensure that they are the same size.

2 Thread an embroidery needle with embroidery thread. Using stab stitch (see page 71) and running stitch, decorate areas of the fabric in different colours of thread.

3 Stitch clusters of buttons in different sizes and shades into and around the embroidered areas. Place them at least 2cm (¾ in.) from the edge of the fabric.

## MAKING UP THE BAG OUTER

1 Place the two pieces wrong sides together and pin the two shortest sides and the bottom edge together. Leave the top edge open.

2 Stitch around the edge of the bag, making sure that you are at least 1cm (⅜ in.) in from the edge and maintaining a straight line.

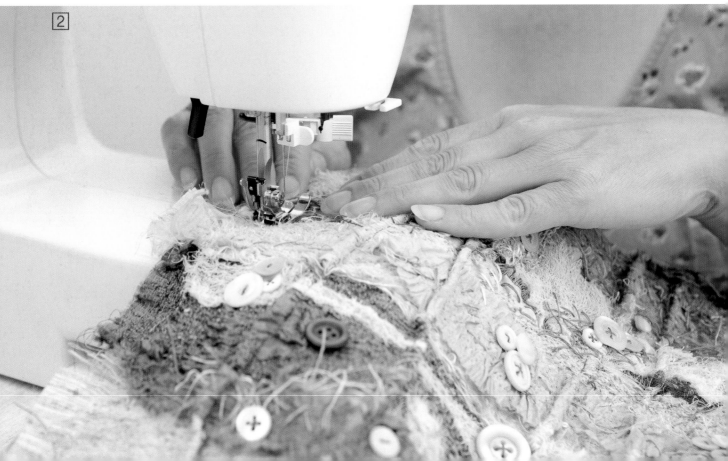

## MAKING UP THE LINING

**1** Right sides facing, fold the lining fabric in half and lay the bag flat on top of it. Cut around the bag to make two pieces of lining fabric the same size. I have cut the fabric so that the top features a frayed edge. Use the sewing machine to stitch around the sides and along the bottom edge of the lining, as for the bag outer.

**2** Place the lining inside the bag, so that the wrong sides are facing. Align the top edges and pin them together.

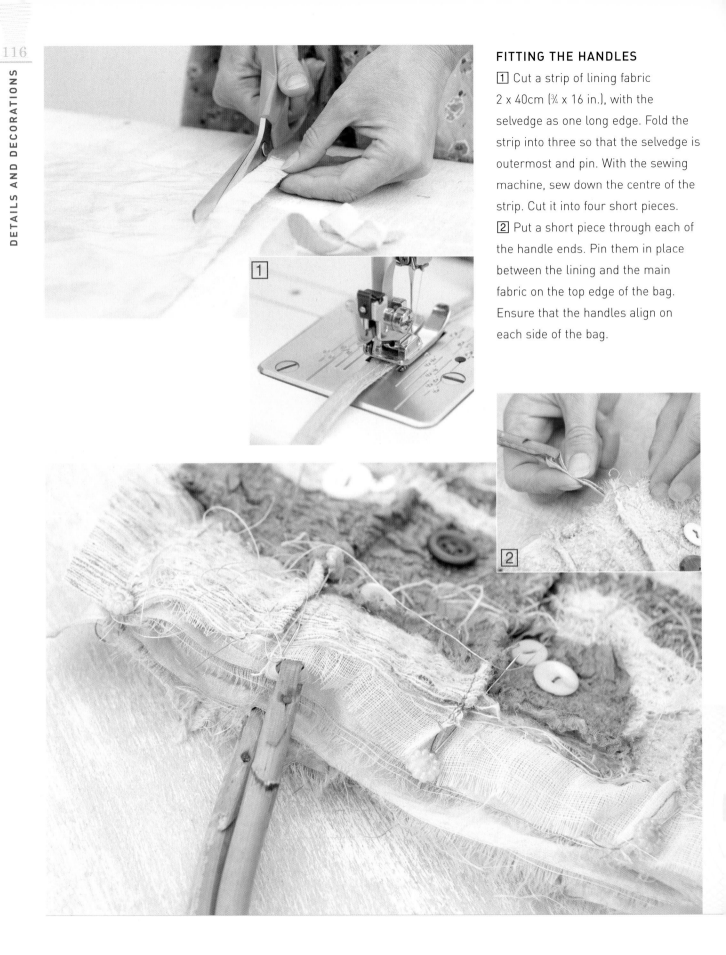

## FITTING THE HANDLES

**1** Cut a strip of lining fabric 2 x 40cm (¾ x 16 in.), with the selvedge as one long edge. Fold the strip into three so that the selvedge is outermost and pin. With the sewing machine, sew down the centre of the strip. Cut it into four short pieces.

**2** Put a short piece through each of the handle ends. Pin them in place between the lining and the main fabric on the top edge of the bag. Ensure that the handles align on each side of the bag.

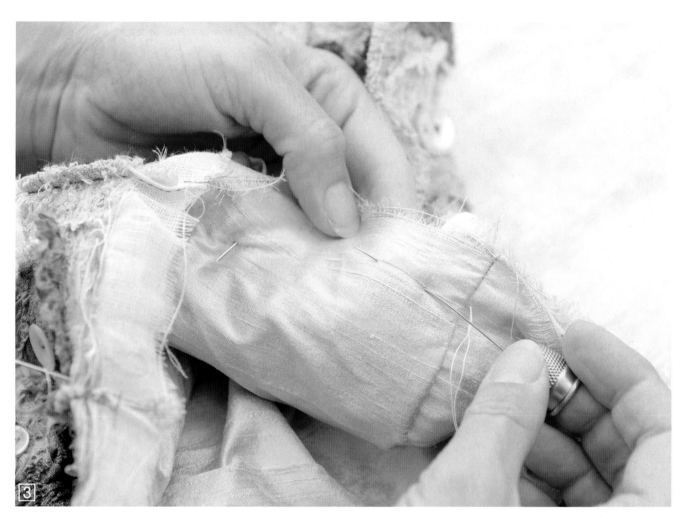

3 Tack around the top edge to hold
everything in place before you
machine stitch.

4 Using straight stitch and matching
thread on the sewing machine, stitch
around the top edge, at least 1cm
(¾ in.) from the edge. Ensure that all
layers are stitched through and
maintain a straight line. Unpick the
tacking stitches.

This appealing bracelet is made from strips of velvet and silk punched together. The punched shot velvet creates a mossy background and the bright dots coming through are reminiscent of flowers against green foliage. This fabric is highlighted with a variety of beads, including bugles and rocailles. You could also usey sequins of various sizes and shapes, or a variety of embroidery stitches over the surface.

# BEADED
## BRACELET

*The embellishing process and beads of various colours and sizes are used to re-create the random dots of colour offered by wild flowers.*

*embellishing inspiration*

## YOU WILL NEED

- ☐ Strip of green shot-silk velvet measuring approximately 30 x 6cm (12 x 2½ in.)
- ☐ Strips of fine silk in pink, orange and green
- ☐ Matching polyester sewing threads
- ☐ Bugle and rocaille beads in toning colours, as well as a few larger shapes

## EQUIPMENT

- ☐ Embellisher machine
- ☐ Tape measure
- ☐ A paint palette to keep your beads organised and ready to use
- ☐ Fabric scissors
- ☐ Hand-sewing needle
- ☐ Beading needle if your beads have small holes

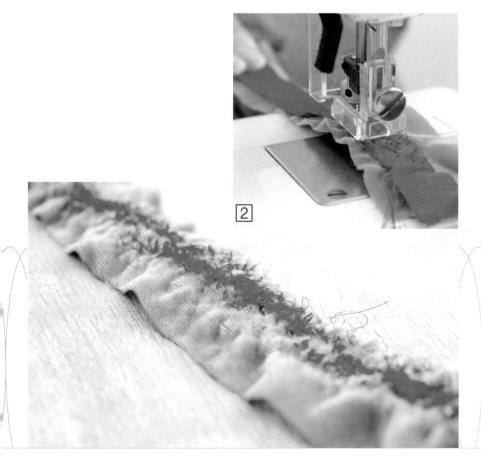

## PREPARING THE FABRIC

1 Measure around the largest part
of your hand. Cut a 6-cm (2½-in.)
wide strip of velvet at least 8cm (3 in.)
longer than this measurement to
allow for shrinkage and overlap.

2 Cut or tear three strips from each
of the other silk fabrics. They will be
overlapped, so each one should
measure about 15–20 x 2–3cm
(6–8 x ¾–1¼ in.). Place one of the silk
strips on the back of the velvet and
punch them together on the
machine. Take care not to over-
punch at this stage; you are aiming
for small, coloured tufts emerging on
the right side of the velvet.

3 Punch the other silk strips onto the back of the velvet in the same way, again being careful not to over-work them.

## FITTING THE BRACELET

1 Fold the long edges of the velvet to the centre and punch again to form a firm strip. Take care not to over-punch and so lose the delicate textures. Don't forget that the stitched-on beads will also help to hold the fabrics together.

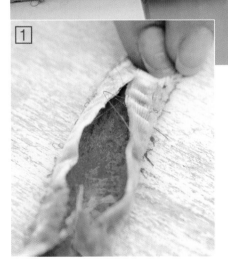

2 Cut the strip to size: it should fit over your hand with enough extra to overlap the ends by about 2cm (¾ in.). Sew the ends together using small hand stitches.

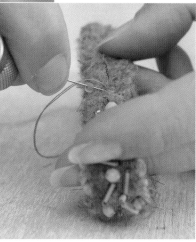

## ADDING BEADS

1 Using polyester sewing thread and a beading needle if necessary, stitch on beads in clusters around the fabric bracelet.

2 Take a small backstitch between each bead to prevent them working loose, then take the needle through to the next bead position. Continue to bead in areas all over the bracelet, in particular over the joined ends.

*This cuff is made in the same way as the bracelet, but the edges have been left frayed for a softer effect.*

## FLOWER SEQUIN GARDEN

The background has been worked in a variety of textured green fabrics – such as velvet, organza and shot dupion – on a felt background. Pink fabric has been punched through from the back to produce dots indicating small flowers. Flower-shaped sequins were secured by beads and the stems were hand-embroidered using stab stitch.

# SAMPLES
## AND IDEAS

## MANIPULATED AND BEADED NECKLACE

Strips of silk and viscose chiffon have been punched together from the front and back. These have then been manipulated onto a felt, oval-shaped backing using hand-stitching to secure the fabrics. The smaller round shapes have been made by winding the strips into balls, again securing them with hand stitches. These pieces have then been stitched together to form a pleasing composition. Various shapes and sizes of beads have been added before stitching the piece onto a cord to tie around the neck.

## PINK BOLLYWOOD RING, EARRINGS AND BARRETTE

The barrette (at the back) has been made in the same way as the necklace, below, using strips of embellished fabric manipulated by hand-stitching them onto a felt base. Sequins and beads have been stitched on and diamanté attached using gemstone or strong fabric glue. A barrette finding has been stitched to the back.

For the ring and earrings, strips of embellished fabrics have been manipulated into balls and then beaded. Tiny diamantés have been attached, using a cocktail stick to apply the glue. The ring mount has also been glued on, while the earrings have had the ear wires stitched in place.

## TYNTESFIELD

This highly textured piece was based on photographs of the wall at Tyntesfield House, an old property near my home. I interpreted the wall, climbing vine and buds with a variety of textile techniques. The embellisher was used to make a textured fabric from linen, silks and scrims. This was manipulated using stitched tucks on the sewing machine. Further manipulation and decoration were created with hand stitches. Bright red buttons added a final touch and represent the buds. This fabric would make a lovely bag in the style of the Lichen Wall Bag, (see page 110).

*embellishing inspiration*

## MACHINE EMBROIDERED SAMPLE

Vintage printed silks have been punched onto a felt background, taking care not to over-work the fabric and so lose some of the texture. The background has then been free-motion embroidered on the sewing machine using viscose embroidery threads.

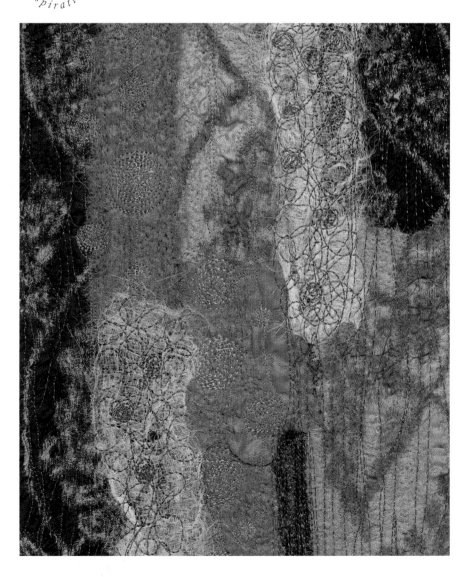

# TEMPLATES

## FOR SIMPLE PUNCHED FABRIC, SEE PAGE 26.

# SUPPLIERS

## EMBELLISHER MACHINE
**Janome UK Ltd**
Janome Centre
Southside
Bredbury
Stockport
Cheshire SK6 2SP
Tel: 0161 666 6004
www.janome-uk.co.uk
The machine I use and that is used in this book is made by Janome.

## FABRICS
**Cloth House**
47 and 98 Berwick Street
London W1F 8SJ
Tel: 010 7437 5155
www.clothhouse.com
Range of fabrics, braids and buttons.

**The Silk Society**
44 Berwick Street
London W1F 0PP
Tel: 020 7287 1881
www.thesilksociety.com
Vast range of silk fabrics.

**The Silk Route**
Cross Cottage
Cross Lane
Frimley Green
Surrey GU16 6LN
Tel: 01252 835781
www.thesilkroute.co.uk
Fabrics, threads and ribbons. Variety packs of different textured and coloured silks.

## EMBROIDERY THREADS AND YARNS
**Silken Strands**
20 Y Rhos
Bangor
Gwynedd LL57 2LT
Tel: 01248 362361
www.silkenstrands.co.uk
Embroidery threads of all kinds.

**Get Knitted**
39 Brislington Hill
Brislington
Bristol BS4 5BE
Tel: 0117 300 5211
www.getknitted.com
Large range of knitting yarns.

**Texere Yarns**
College Mill
Barkerend Road
Bradford BD1 4AU
Tel: 01274 722191
www.texere.co.uk
Yarns, fibres and threads.

## FIBRES
**Wingham Wools**
70 Main Street
Wentworth
Rotherham
South Yorkshire S62 7TN
Tel: 01226 742926
www.winghamwolls.com
Felt-making materials, fibres and yarns.

**Art Van Go**
The Studios
1 Stevenage Road
Knebworth
Hertfordshire SG3 6AN
Tel: 01438 814946
art@artvango.co.uk
Angelina fibres and some fabrics.

## BEADS AND JEWELLERY FINDINGS
**Fred Aldous Ltd**
37 Lever Street
Manchester M1 1LW
Tel: 0161 236 4224
www.fredaldous.co.uk
Jewellery findings such as brooch backs and barrettes.

**Bijoux Beads**
2 Abbey Street
Bath BA1 1NN
Tel: 01225 482024
www.bijouxbeads.co.uk
Beads and jewellery findings.

**Creative Beadcraft**
Unit 2 Asheridge Business Centre
Asheridge Road
Chesham
Bucks HP5 2PT
Tel: 01494 778818
www.creativebeadcraft.co.uk
Diamante, beads and jewellery findings.

## ACKNOWLEDGEMENTS
Thanks to:
Lynn Snow and Di Goodison for introducing me to this amazing machine.
Michael Wicks for the beautiful and inspiring photographs. The model, Naomi Childs.
Elizabeth Healey for the creative book design.
All at Breslich & Foss for their support and encouragement throughout the project. It is very much appreciated.
Steve, my partner of 20 years, for your support and love through yet another book project. Thanks for putting up with my insane working hours for all these years and for the use of your painting as inspiration for the magenta flower garden cushion.

# INDEX